Learning Unlimited®

let's play recorder
LEVEL ONE INSTRUCTION

HAL•LEONARD® CORPORATION

7777 W. BLUEMOUND RD. P.O. BOX 13819 MILWAUKEE, WI 53213

Acknowledgments

To Professor Walter Gerboth, Brooklyn College, for his advice and assistance.

To Professor Paul Glass and his publishers, GROSSET AND DUNLAP for granting permission to reprint material from "Songs Of The West."

To B.A. Kalanzi for permission to include his African song "Kawa."

To David Ormont for his creative lyrics.

To Paula Sue Ober, for her comments and suggestions.

Dedicated to, and for, Wolf.

introduction

You're about to enjoy a fabulous new experience – playing a musical instrument! The recorder is easy to use and, with the aid of your teacher and the LET'S PLAY RECORDER INSTRUCTION BOOKLET, you'll soon master the basics of playing.

In addition to instruction and exercises, Level One provides you with plenty of opportunity to apply what you learn by playing dozens of your favorite songs, arranged as solos, duets and ensembles. And as you play and learn, the whole world of music opens before you.

Ready? Let's play recorder!

let's look at the recorder

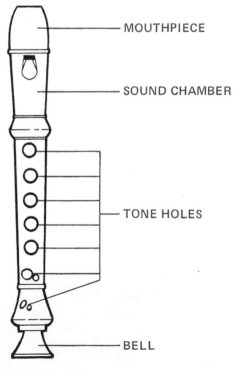

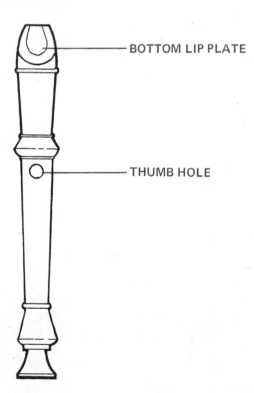

FRONT VIEW   BACK VIEW

MOUTHPIECE

SOUND CHAMBER

TONE HOLES

BELL

BOTTOM LIP PLATE

THUMB HOLE

it's easy to get a tone!

step 1.

Hold the recorder with your right hand around the bell. The tone holes should be facing toward the ceiling.

step 2.

Place the lip plate of the recorder on your lower lip. Make sure your lower lip is resting on your lower teeth.

step 3.

Bring your top lip gently down on the tip of the mouthpiece and slightly tighten the corners of your mouth.

step 4.

Sit up straight with your feet flat on the floor. Take a natural breath and blow softly into the recorder as if whispering the word "too ——".

fingering

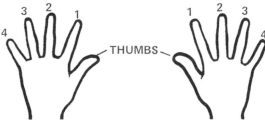

LEFT HAND   RIGHT HAND

With your left thumb, cover the thumb hole on the back side of the recorder. Cover the top three tone holes with the first, second, and third fingers of your left hand. Cover the lower tone holes with your first, second, third and fourth right-hand fingers.

your first note...B

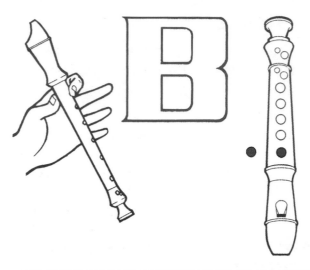

- With your left thumb, cover the thumb hole on the recorder.

- With your first finger, cover the top hole on the front side of the recorder.

- Now, to play B, softly whisper the "too" sound into the recorder and hold it.

- Play B over and over, holding it each time you play it.

Now tap your foot as you play the note B. Each tap is called a beat.

1 1 beat (tap) for each note.
TAP | | | | | | | |
PLAY B B B B B B B B

2 2 beats (taps) for each note.
TAP | | | | | | | |
PLAY B ▬ B ▬ B ▬ B ▬

3 3 beats (taps) for each note.
TAP | | | | | | | |
PLAY B ▬▬ B ▬▬

4 4 beats (taps) for each note.
TAP | | | | | | | |
PLAY B ▬▬▬ B ▬▬▬

silent beats are called rests

𝄽 This is called a one beat rest. (It is also called a quarter rest). It means that on that beat, you tap your foot but do not play.

1 TAP | | | | | | | | | | | | | | | |
PLAY B B B 𝄽 B B 𝄽 B B 𝄽 B B B ▬▬ B

2 TAP | | | | | | | | | | | | | | | |
PLAY B B ▬ 𝄽 𝄽 B B ▬ 𝄽 𝄽 B 𝄽 B 𝄽 B ▬ 𝄽

4

your second note...A

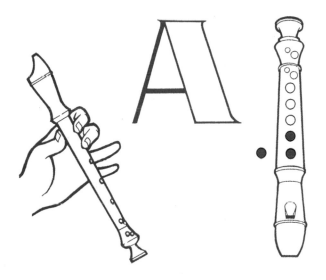

- Cover the thumb hole and the first two holes of the recorder as shown in the diagram.

- Be sure to curve your fingers and cover the holes firmly.

- Take a natural breath and hold.

- Now, softly play the new note A and hold.

- Play the note A several times and then play the note B several times.

let's play

Play each of the following phrases four times without stopping.

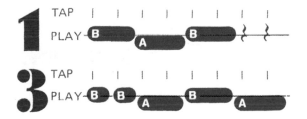

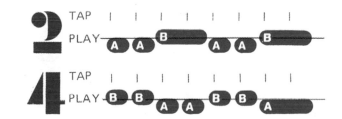

repeat signs :‖

When you come to a repeat sign at the end of a phrase, go back to the beginning of the phrase and play it once again.

Try the following phrase using the repeat sign

measures and bar lines

From now on, each line of music will be divided into smaller sections by bar lines, as shown in the example to the right. The sections between the bar lines are called measures.

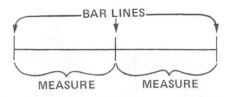

meter signature

The number placed at the beginning of each song tells you the number of beats there are in each measure of that song.

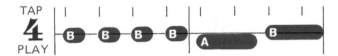

let's play some different rhythms

mambo

waltz

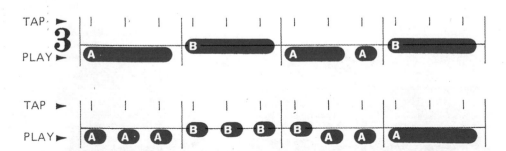

your third note...G

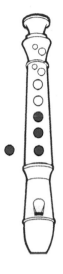

- Cover the thumb hole and the first three holes of the recorder as shown in the diagram.

- Be sure to curve your fingers and cover the tone holes firmly.

- Sit up straight, with your feet flat on the floor.

- Take a natural breath and hold.

- Softly play the new tone G and hold it.

- Play G several times and then play A and B.

it's fun to read music!

the staff

Notes are written on a staff — five lines and the four spaces between them. Each line and space has its own letter name. You can tell the name of a note by the name of the line or space it's on.

STAFF

the treble clef sign

At the beginning of each staff is a "treble clef sign," also called a "G clef." This sign tells you that the second line of the staff is called "G".

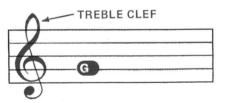
TREBLE CLEF

the musical alphabet

Musical tones are named after the first seven letters of the alphabet: A, B, C, D, E, F, and G. After the note G you start over with A, B, and so on. So far you know three notes: G, A, and B. You'll learn more about the other notes as you learn to play them.

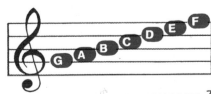
MUSICAL ALPHABET 7

let's play B, A, G

A double bar indicates the end of a line of music.

practice themes

Practice themes are short melodies which will help improve your playing. Repeat these themes several times, until you can play them without any hesitation. Then have fun playing them without looking at the music.

1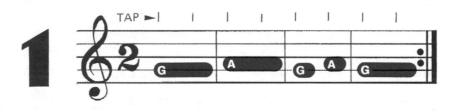

2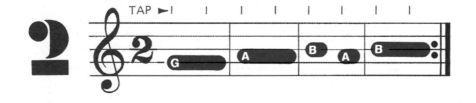

3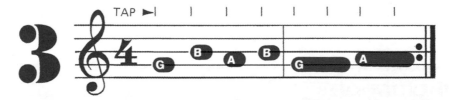

here's help
As you play the practice themes, check these points:

- Are your fingers covering the holes firmly?
- Does the tone sound pleasant?
- Are the tones coming out clearly?

- Are you starting each tone on time?
- Are you holding the long tones?
- Are you whispering the sound "too" for each tone?

peace must be our goal

SEVUSH-ORMONT

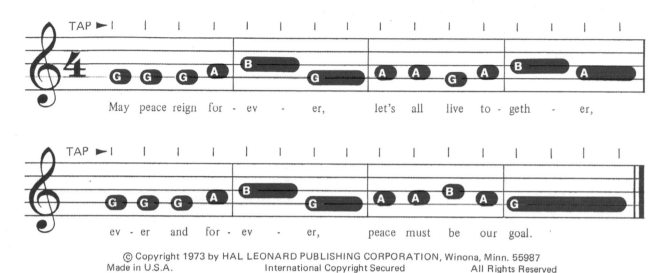

May peace reign for - ev - er, let's all live to - geth - er,

ev - er and for - ev - er, peace must be our goal.

miasama* ...FROM THE MIKADO

GILBERT-SULLIVAN

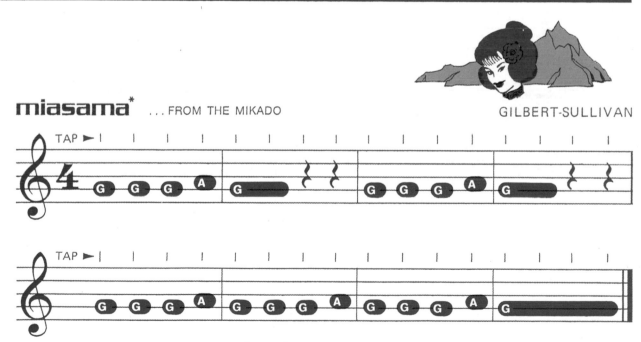

*This melody can be accompanied by triangles and hand cymbals.

reading standard music notation

Every note written on the staff tells you two specific things:
- The appearance of a note tells you how many beats it receives.
- Its placement on the staff tells you its name (review the musical alphabet on page 7).

1 quarter note

The quarter note looks like this ♩ or ♩ and receives one beat.

Let's place the quarter note on the staff.

2 half note

The half note looks like this 𝅗𝅥 or 𝅗𝅥 and receives two beats.

Let's place the half note on the staff.

HALF REST — Denotes two beats of silence.

3 dotted half note

The dotted half note looks like this 𝅗𝅥. or 𝅗𝅥. and receives three beats.

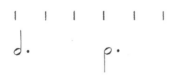

Let's place the dotted half note on the staff.

4 whole note

The whole note looks like this 𝅝 and receives four beats.

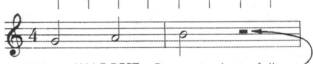

Now, let's place the whole note on the staff.

WHOLE REST — Denotes four beats of silence.

time signature

At the beginning of every song, you will now see a set of two numbers. These numbers are called a time signature (also called meter signature).

$$\frac{4}{4}, \frac{3}{4}, \frac{2}{4}$$

— the top number indicates the number of beats in each measure.

— the bottom number indicates the kind of note that receives one beat (¼ or quarter note).

let's play some songs using notation

merrily we roll along

solo flight

windy day waltz

cuckoo

adding the new note...C

- Cover the thumbhole with your left thumb, and cover the second hole of the recorder with your left middle finger.
- Sit up straight, with your feet on the floor.
- Take a natural breath and hold it.
- Softly play C and hold it.
- Play C several times and then practice moving back and forth from C to the other notes you know.

practice themes

march tempo

calypso beat

la conga

waltz

blue birch bark canoe...

Try playing a rhythm accompaniment for this song by tapping a tom-tom on each beat indicated by this symbol ♩.

SEVUSH-ORMONT

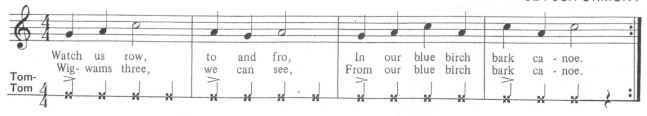

12

the tie

The tie is a curved line that connects two or more notes of the same pitch. It indicates that, instead of playing the note twice, you play the first note and hold it for the total time value of both notes.

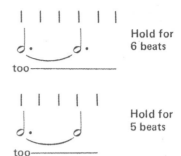

Hold for 6 beats

too

Hold for 5 beats

too

practice saying these tied rhythms

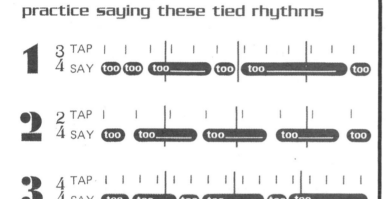

practice playing these tied rhythms

i'd like to know

SEVUSH-ORMONT

In the seventh and eighth measures, hold the tied A's for 5 full beats. Can you find another tie in this song?

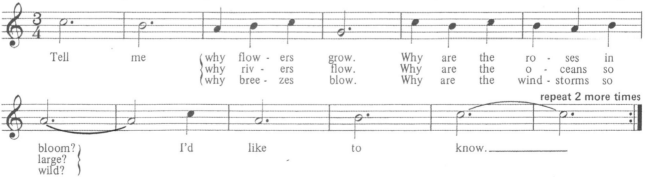

Tell me why flow-ers grow. Why are the ro-ses in
why riv-ers flow. Why are the o-ceans so
why bree-zes blow. Why are the wind-storms so

bloom?
large?
wild?

I'd like to know.

repeat 2 more times

let's play a duet!

This song is a duet, a song that can be played by two people at the same time. Try this duet with someone who plays a recorder. One of you play Part A while the other plays Part B.

russian march

SEVUSH-ORMONT

The new symbol at the end of this song is called a fermata sign ⌢. When a fermata sign appears over a note, hold that note slightly longer than its actual time value.

Written:

Played: too ____

a new note...D

- Cover the second hole with your left middle finger.
- Be sure that the thumb hole is open.
- Sit up straight, with your feet on the floor.
- Take a natural breath and softly play D and hold it.
- Play D several times, and then practice moving back and forth from D to the other notes you know.

finger breakers

The following exercises will help you learn the new note D. Start by playing each one slowly and smoothly. As you gain confidence, gradually increase your speed.

shadows fall

SEVUSH-ORMONT

Sha - dows fall,_____ Hear the crick - ets call,_____ Dark-ness cov- er- ing all as eve- ning sha- dows fall. _____

playing smoothly..."legato"

A curved line that connects two or more notes of different pitch is called a slur. All the notes within a slur are to be played legato , or, smoothly.

So far, you've been starting each note with a "too" sound. From now on, when you see a group of notes connected by a slur, start only the first note with "too". Then continue the same "oo——" sound for the rest of the notes within the slur.

SLUR

"legato" melody

chorale
BEETHOVEN'S 9th SYMPHONY

etude

An etude is a song which will help you learn a particular technique. This etude will help you learn how to play slurs which extend across bar lines.

16

calypso...*duet*

SEVUSH-
ORMONT

With Calypso Beat

Trin - i - dad,____ Trin - i - dad,____ When I'm here, when you're near, I'm so

glad____ Trin - i - dad,____ Trin - i - dad,____ When a - way, for a

day, I am sad,____ Miss you so____ When I go____ I feel

blue, be - cause of you____ Trin - i - dad____ Trin - i - dad.

eighth notes

All of the notes you've learned so far have been held for at least one beat. Eighth notes are held for only one-half beat. This means that it takes two eighth notes to make one full beat.

Tap and say the first four measures of the song "Jingle Bells" shown below. Notice that for each pair of eighth notes , you tap only once.

counting eighth notes

In the example above, each note had its own syllable, making it easy to say the rhythm of the song aloud. From now on, whenever there are eighth notes in a song, say the syllable "ti" for each eighth note, and "ta" for all other notes.

The melody in the example below is again "Jingle Bells", but the words have been changed to "ti" and "ta". Tap and say this example aloud.

check out: Write in "ti" or "ta" under each note. ———————————

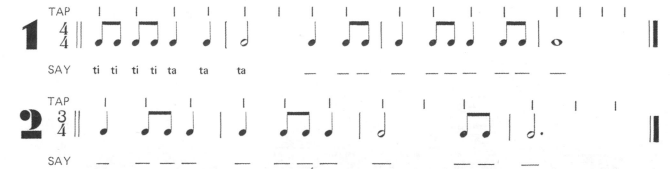

Play the two rhythm lines above on your recorder, using the note B. Then play them again, using any notes you wish. Compose your own rhythm piece using eighth notes.

18

lightly row

Light - ly row   light - ly row   on the glass - y   waves we go,

smooth - ly glide,   smooth - ly glide,   on the si - lent tide.

the round

A ROUND is a song in which two groups play the same melody, starting at different times. For this round, your instructor will divide your class into two groups. The first group will begin the song at A. When they reach B, the second group will begin at A. Then both groups will continue playing until they reach the end of the song.

down at the station

Down   at the   sta - tion   ear - ly in the   morn - ing,

See the   lit - tle   puf - fer   bil - lies   lined up in a   row,

See the   en - gine   dri - ver   pull the   lit - tle   throt - tle

Puff,   puff,   choo,   choo,   off they   go.

the note F

There are two fingerings which may be used for the note F. Ask your teacher which fingering you should use.

- Cover the first three holes, as you did for the note G.
- Place your right thumb directly behind the F hole.
- Cover the F hole with your right index finger as shown below.

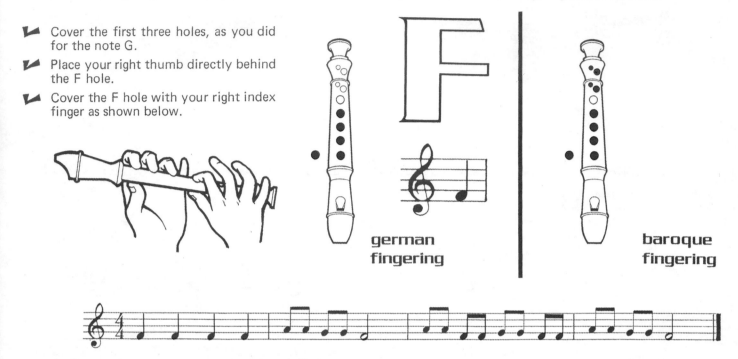

german fingering

baroque fingering

let's learn to play staccato

A staccato mark (•) placed above or below a note tells you to play that note short and crisp. Simply stop the flow of air, do NOT stop the "too" sound with your tongue as if saying "toot".

pins and needles

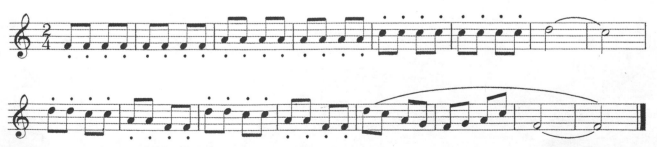

march staccato

SEVUSH-ORMONT

Would I go to the coun - try, where I'd swim and ride on a horse? Would I

like to play all the live - long day? Why of course, why of course, why of course I would!

shortnin' bread

C means Common Time and is played the same as $\frac{4}{4}$ — that is, 4 beats per measure, a quarter note receives 1 beat.

Three lit - tle chil - dren ly - ing in bed, Two was sick and the oth - er near dead!

Sent for the doc - tor, doc - tor said, "Feed them chil - dren some

short - nin' bread." Mom - my's lit - tle ba - by loves short - nin', short - nin',

Mom - my's lit - tle ba - by loves short - nin' bread. Mom - my's lit - tle ba - by loves

short - nin', short - nin', Mom - my's lit - tle ba - by loves short - nin' bread.

pick-up notes

Sometimes the first measure of a song doesn't have a complete number of beats. The missing beats are found in the last measure. The notes in the incomplete first measure are called pick-up notes

a tisket a tasket

---

the dotted quarter note

A dot after a note increases the time value of that note by one-half. Therefore, a dotted quarter note receives 1½ beats.

A dotted quarter note is usually followed by an eighth note. In the example to the right notice that the dotted quarter note is held through the first half of the second beat. The eighth note comes in on the last half of the second beat.

Count this rhythm using "ta" and "ti".

michael, row the boat ashore

two new notes...E and D

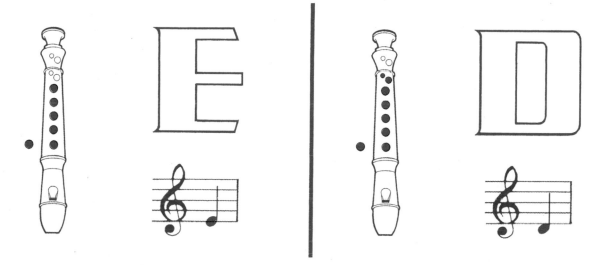

etudes using E and D

When playing low tones such as D and E, play more softly, open your embouchure as you move into the lower register, and use the sound "doo" instead of "too".

let's improvise

To improvise, you make up a new version of a familiar song by changing the rhythm or melody. It's like telling a familiar story, but changing the details to make it more interesting.

Improvisations are not written. You simply make them up as you go along, using your "ears" to guide you. As you improvise, remember to "hear" the music you are improvising on.

To begin improvising, create a rhythm pattern with words, using any sentence you wish. As an example we'll use the sentence, "I love to go to school". Clap a steady beat and say the word pattern over and over until you have performed it a dozen different ways. Each time you say it differently you are improvising.

Improvise on "I love to go to school" to create several different feelings or moods. Perform this word pattern as if you

1. don't like to go to school
2. love to go to school
3. whisper in school

4. are happy in school
5. tip-toe in school

DON'T GO ON UNTIL YOU HAVE COMPLETED EACH OF THE 5 EXERCISES ABOVE.

Tap and say the following improvised rhythms of the word pattern "I love to go to school."

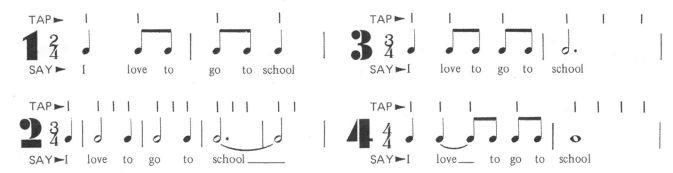

Now play the rhythm of the above examples and your own word patterns on the recorder, using the note G.

As you play your word patterns over and over, change the mood (improvise) by playing each pattern a) smoothly   b) staccato   c) starting softly and becoming louder (crescendo)   d) starting loudly and becoming softer.

using more notes to improvise

Improvise with two notes, E and G, on the word pattern "I love to go to school".
As shown in the examples below, you can start with either note.

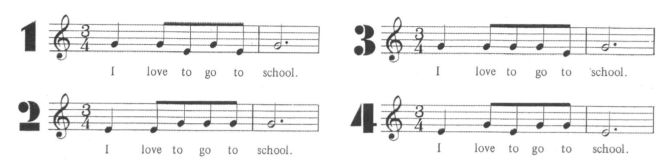

1 I love to go to school.

2 I love to go to school.

3 I love to go to school.

4 I love to go to school.

remember:
These examples are written out to help explain improvising. DO NOT read music when you improvise. Play what you feel at that moment. If you wish, play your word patterns differently each time. Keep "hearing" the word pattern for each rhythm.

Now add the note A to the notes E and G for your improvisations. See how many different ways you can play the same word pattern with these three tones.

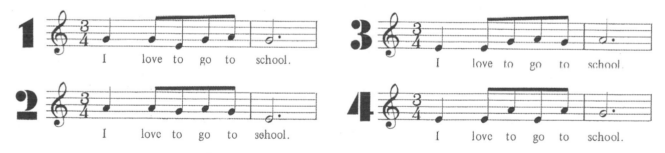

1 I love to go to school.

2 I love to go to school.

3 I love to go to school.

4 I love to go to school.

now you're on your own...*experiment and create*

- ✔ Gradually add more tones to your improvisations.
- ✔ Experiment with mood effects (legato, staccato, crescendo etc.)
- ✔ Create longer word patterns for more interesting rhythms.
- ✔ Add improvised rhythm band accompaniments.

25

a new note...low C

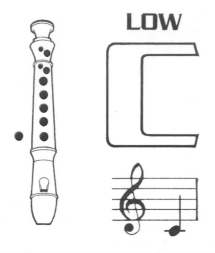

LOW C

Low C is the lowest note on the soprano recorder, and may at first be difficult to play. For C and other low notes, follow these suggestions:

- Blow very softly into the recorder.
- Make sure all the holes are covered firmly.
- Play on the tip of the mouthpiece.
- Slightly relax the corners of your mouth.

chords

When three or more tones are played at once, they produce a chord. The main note in each chord gives the chord its name: for example, the C chord, or the G chord. Many accompaniment parts are made up of chords.

Although it is not possible to play full chords on the recorder, you can give the effect of a chord by playing the notes of the chord one at a time. Chords played in this manner are called broken chords

The colored notes at the beginning of each exercise below are the tones of the chord indicated above the staff. In each exercise, you'll be playing these tones as broken chords. Practice each exercise until you can play it quickly, smoothly, and accurately.

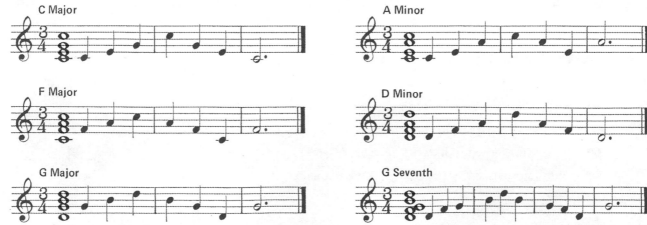

C Major

A Minor

F Major

D Minor

G Major

G Seventh

using broken chords *to accompany the voice*

weeping willows

The recorder and voice blend beautifully together, as you'll hear when you play this duet with some of your friends. In this song, the voice sings the melody on the syllable "Lu", while the recorder plays a broken chord accompaniment.

1st and 2nd endings

jingle bells

To play this song, start at the beginning and play to the repeat sign in the bracketed 1st ending. Then repeat from the beginning of the song. This time, skip the 1st ending and play the 2nd ending instead.

sweet betsy from pike

Repeat from this sign instead of from the very beginning.

Oh, don't you re-mem-ber sweet Bet-sy from Pike, Who crossed the big
even-ing quite ear-ly they camped on the Platte, 'Twas near by a

moun-tains with her lov-er Ike, With two yoke of ox-en, a large yal-ler
tree in a green sha-dy flat, When Bet-sy so tir-ed lay down to re-

dog, A____ tall Shang-hai roost-er and one spot-ted hog? Sing____
pose And____ Ike, he gazed down on his Pike coun-ty Rose.

Chorus

ho-di-dee du-di-dee ho-di-dee day. Sing____ ho-di-dee

du-di-dee ho-di-dee day. 2. One ho-di-dee day.

28

chord accompaniment... *for sweet betsy from pike*

Sweet Betsy From Pike can also be played as a Quartet, a song played by four people at once. One person plays the melody on the preceding page and each of the others play line A, B, or C below. For some real fun, have three of your friends join you. The letters above the staff indicate the chords used in the accompaniment part.

a new note...B♭ (B flat)

A flat (♭) lowers the pitch of a note. A flat placed before a note affects all notes on the same line or space which follow in that measure.

finger breakers

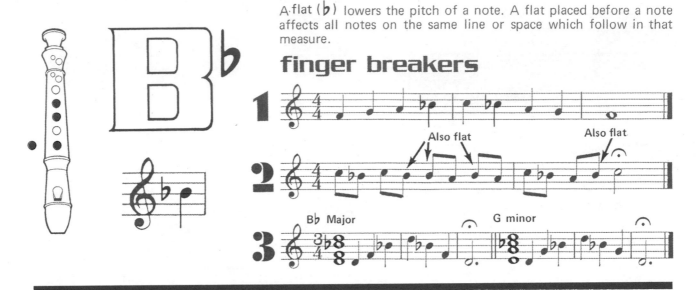

theme by borodin

When all the B's in a song are to be played flat, the flat is written only once, at the beginning of the song, between the treble clef and the time signature. This flat is called a key signature.

a new time signature...⁶⁄₈

As you've already learned, the top number of a time signature indicates the number of beats per measure, and the bottom number indicates the type of note that receives one beat.

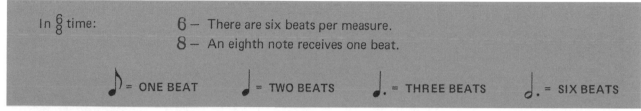

In ⁶⁄₈ time:

6 – There are six beats per measure.

8 – An eighth note receives one beat.

♪ = ONE BEAT   ♩ = TWO BEATS   ♩. = THREE BEATS   ♩. = SIX BEATS

looby loo

1 2 3 4 5 6

another way of counting ⁶⁄₈ time

When a song in ⁶⁄₈ time is played fast, it is too difficult to tap and count six beats in each measure. Instead, tap only on beats ONE and FOUR, and feel the rhythm in two large beats. Tap and count this exercise with two beats per measure.

Counted in six: 1   2   3   4   5   6
Counted in two: 1   -   -   2   -   -

irish washerwoman

- - 1 - - 2 - -

a new note...F♯ (F sharp)

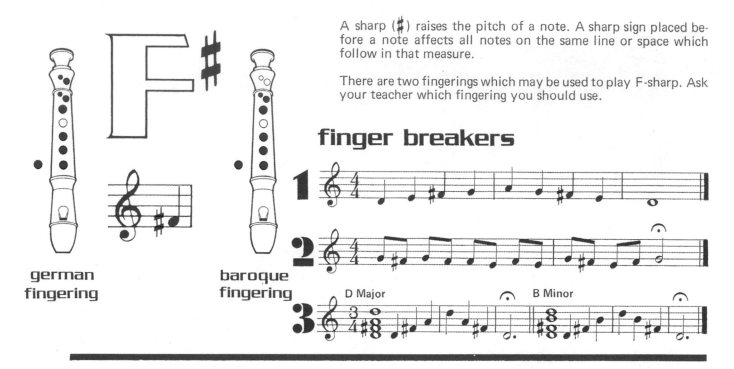

german fingering

baroque fingering

A sharp (♯) raises the pitch of a note. A sharp sign placed before a note affects all notes on the same line or space which follow in that measure.

There are two fingerings which may be used to play F-sharp. Ask your teacher which fingering you should use.

finger breakers

down in the valley

When a sharp appears on the top line in the key signature, play every F in the song as F-sharp.

D.S. and D.C.

D.S. al Fine. . .When you come to D.S. al Fine in the music,
go back to the sign 𝄋 and repeat to the word Fine.

bella bimba

Italian Folk Song

D.C. al Fine. . .When you come to D.C. al Fine in a song,
go back to the beginning and repeat to the word Fine.

el florón

Folk Song from Puerto Rico

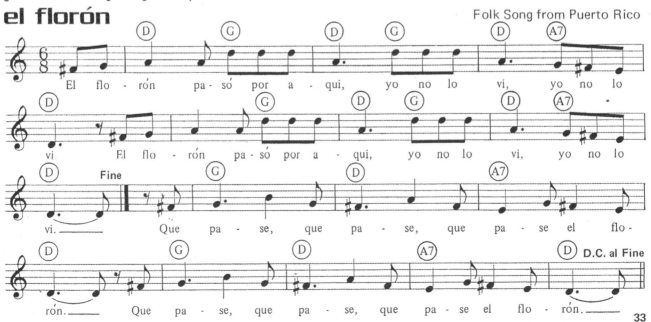

kawa...*an african answer song*

Throughout this song you'll see dotted quarter rests 𝄽. In ⁶⁄₈ time, this kind of rest is equal to three whole beats of silence.   𝄽 = 3 Beats of Silence

To make this song even more exciting, add a drumbeat each time you see this symbol in the music.

In this melody from Uganda, Africa, the leader sings out and the chorus answers.

by B.A. KALANZI

*Pronounced "moo-noo-nu-inġ-ga"

dynamics

Dynamic markings indicate how loudly or softly you are to play. The most common dynamics are:

pp	very soft	*mf*	medium loud
p	soft	*f*	loud
mp	medium soft	*ff*	very loud

Crescendo is an Italian word that means "to grow louder". In music it is usually abbreviated cresc. or ⟨

The Italian word Decrescendo means "to grow softer". Its abbreviation is decresc. or ⟩

dona nobis pacem*

Get together with some of your friends and play this song in three parts, as you did in "Down At The Station" on page 19.

Be sure to pay close attention to the dynamic marks in this song.

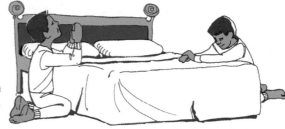

Early Latin Canon

* The Latin words are pronounced "doh́ nah nó - bees pah́ - chem", and mean, "Grant us peace".

bingo

American Folk Song

Farm - er Brown he had a dog and Bin - go was his name - o. B - I - N - G - O,

B - I - N - G - O, B - I - N - G - O, and Bin - go was his name - o.

zum gali gali

Israeli Folk Song

The song "Zum Gali Gali" is another arrangement written for two recorders. The rit. sign in the last measure is an abbreviation for the word ritard and means to become gradually slower.

(Melody) Introduction

(Chant)

Zum ga - li ga - li ga - li, Zum ga - li ga - li, Zum ga - li ga - li ga - li, Zum ga - li ga - li,

He - cha - lutz I' maan a - vo - dah; A - vo - dah I' maan he - cha - lutz.

Zum ga - li ga - li ga - li, Zum ga - li ga - li, Zum ga - li ga - li ga - li, Zum ga - li ga - li,

Zum ga - li ga - li ga - li, Zum ga - li ga - li, Zum ga - li ga - li ga - li, Zum ga - li ga - li.

¢...alla breve or cut time

Cut time ¢ is the symbol for a new time signature, $\frac{2}{2}$. In $\frac{2}{2}$ time, each note receives only half the time value it would receive in $\frac{4}{4}$ time.

¢ or $\frac{2}{2}$ — Two beats per measure
— A half note receives one beat.

jolly old st. nicholas

the army song

the nutcracker suite

overture

march

dance of the reed flutes

chinese dance

waltz of the flowers

waltz of the flowers *(continued)*